Young Adult Literature
Dystopian Worlds

Kiley E. Smith

Contributing Author
Emily Rossman Smith

Consultants
Timothy Rasinski, Ph.D.
Kent State University

Lori Oczkus, M.A.
Literacy Consultant

Publishing Credits
Rachelle Cracchiolo, M.S.Ed., *Publisher*
Conni Medina, M.A.Ed., *Managing Editor*
Dona Herweck Rice, *Series Developer*
Emily R. Smith, M.A.Ed., *Content Director*
Stephanie Bernard and Susan Daddis, *Editors*
Robin Erickson, *Multimedia Designer*

The TIME logo is a registered trademark of TIME Inc. Used under license.

Image Credits: pp.20–21 illustration by Timothy J. Bradley; All other images from iStock and/or Shutterstock.

Teacher Created Materials
5301 Oceanus Drive
Huntington Beach, CA 92649-1030
http://www.tcmpub.com
ISBN 978-1-4938-3599-7
© 2017 Teacher Created Materials, Inc.

Table of Contents

Dystopia, Utopia, Huh-Topia!? 4
Controlling Governments 12
Rebellious Teens 16
Mind Control Backfires 22
The Spark That Triggers the End 26
Who Knows What's Out There? 30
Where in the Real World? 36
All's Fair in War and Utopia 42
Glossary 44
Index 45
Check It Out 46
Try It! 47
About the Author 48

Dystopia, Utopia, Huh-Topia!?

What is a **dystopia**? It is a perfectly horrid society. Civilization's problems have taken over. **Discord** and unhappiness are common. Governments try to create perfect worlds, but something goes wrong. They end up with deeply troubled societies. To paraphrase the great author Leo Tolstoy, each dystopian world is unique. Yet the people are similarly unhappy.

On the other side of the coin are **utopias**. These are perfect societies. The governments are strong and fair. People are treated equally. They are well cared for. Utopian societies produce happy, loving, caring people.

Authors seem to have it backwards! Utopian societies include perfection, peace, and **prosperity**. These are ideal conditions. So why aren't authors writing more utopian books? Wouldn't it be more interesting to read about perfect worlds?

Not really. Utopia by definition has no conflict. Without conflict, there is no story. Dystopian novels focus on one of the most engaging types of conflict. More often than not, they tell of a single person against forces in the outside world. Teenagers are noted for feeling that they face the world alone. Maybe that's why dystopian books are among the most popular novels for young adults.

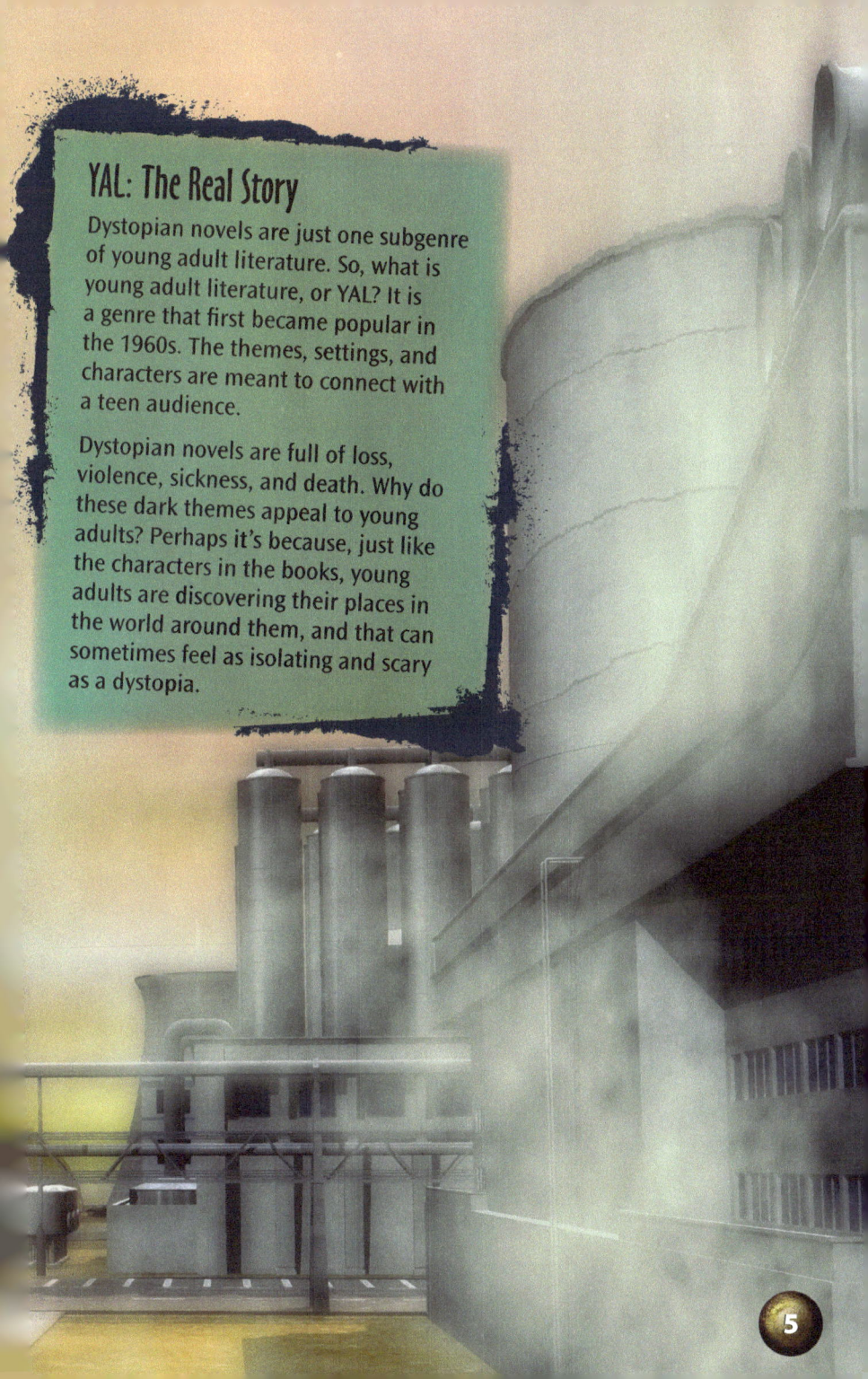

YAL: The Real Story

Dystopian novels are just one subgenre of young adult literature. So, what is young adult literature, or YAL? It is a genre that first became popular in the 1960s. The themes, settings, and characters are meant to connect with a teen audience.

Dystopian novels are full of loss, violence, sickness, and death. Why do these dark themes appeal to young adults? Perhaps it's because, just like the characters in the books, young adults are discovering their places in the world around them, and that can sometimes feel as isolating and scary as a dystopia.

Conflict

All great stories have conflict. Without conflict, there is nothing to help build excitement and interest. Dystopian stories are no different.

In these novels, the main characters, or **protagonists**, usually find themselves in conflict with the greater world. In an individual versus society conflict, the main character is hated by the government or by other people. He or she is seen as a threat to the routine way of life that people are used to. This scares people. The angry government leaders fight the threat by kidnapping or getting rid of the individual.

The dystopian world might also involve an individual in conflict with nature. In such a conflict, the main character is fighting a problem that can't be solved

easily. The only **foreseeable** solution is finding a safe place that provides the **necessities** of life.

In an individual vs. self conflict, the protagonist fights the beasts within. This may be a battle with his or her own self-consciousness. Victory can only come by fighting the protagonist's own dysfunctions. This type of conflict is usually not central to a dystopian novel. These books most often deal with outside forces. But a protagonist may have to overcome his or her own flaws. Such flaws are at the heart of inner conflict.

Dystopia's Conflicts

Dystopian novels have central conflicts that usually fall in one of two main categories:

Individual vs. Society—In *Cinder*, by Marissa Meyer, the protagonist is a cyborg. As the book begins, it becomes clear that cyborgs are treated as second-class citizens in this dystopian society. Cinder is a cyborg fighting against her society.

Individual vs. Nature—In James Dashner's *The Scorch Trials*, nature causes major problems. A terrible disease and the extraordinary heat of the sun cause the destruction of the modern world. The protagonist, Thomas, fights against natural and human enemies.

Elements of Dystopian Worlds

Throughout young adult dystopian novels, there are recurring core themes and ideas. Name any dystopian novel, and you'll find these elements!

Fight
The universe is broken.
It has been shattered by people
who believe in power and control.
They are corrupt and evil.
A few people fight back.
They want to save the
destroyed, crumbling society—
but not always for the same reasons.

Survive
Surviving means to live another day
and see another sunrise.
Protagonists want to survive,
and they want their friends to survive.
Survival is what keeps them fighting
against the dystopian world.

Protect
The ones they love inspire protagonists
to strike back and protect those around them.
They fight to keep everyone safe and
want their families to live in peace.
The world changes because protagonists
love their families.

Change
Not many people have changed the world or even changed their communities. Changing society is a force that pushes people to greatness. Protagonists want to change society, but they end up changing the world.

Love
Love is the most powerful, beautiful force in the universe. Love for family, friends, and others motivates protagonists. They fight back against a world that is anything but perfect.

Finish
All these protagonists fight governments that try to keep them in the dark. They discover truths, and they fight for many reasons. Above all, they fight to end their own dystopias once and for all.

Dystopian Roadmap

Most dystopian novels follow this plot path from dystopia to a new world.

World-Changing Events

A dystopian society is formed after a cataclysmic event.

Born Leaders

The natural leaders within the community begin to emerge and find support.

Life-Changing Moment

The protagonist faces a crisis that changes his or her life forever.

Rebellion

The people join together and rebel against the dystopian forces.

New World Emerges

Decision to Fight

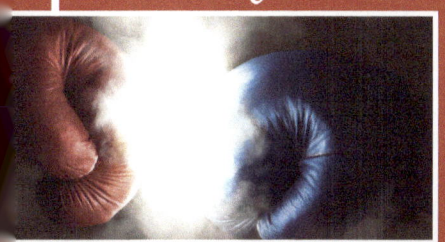

At a key point in the story, the protagonist realizes that fighting is the only way to create change.

In the end, life has been forever changed and a new world begins.

Controlling Governments

In many dystopian novels, leaders try to make perfect worlds but fail. Instead, they create flawed worlds. This often happens because the controlling powers are **corrupt**. They focus on their own needs and ignore the needs of the masses.

There are many different ways governments become corrupt. Some governments are only under the rule of one person who has complete power. Other governments involve a group of villains who work together to gain total control. Controlling governments keep citizens in the dark. The leaders act as if the world is perfect, but it is far from it. These corrupt actions cause people to rebel, and the government fights back. This game of cat and mouse creates dystopian worlds.

Governments also lie to citizens about the outside world. Dystopian leaders often **conceal** the truth about conditions on Earth. They don't want citizens to realize how harsh nature can be. However, with so many people trapped in small areas, problems spread rapidly.

When natural disasters do threaten, people rely on one another to survive. Citizens in these failing worlds are stretched thin. They search for safe places and protection from the elements. Without support from honest leaders, problems arise.

Utopian Society? Yeah, Right.

Lois Lowry's *The Giver* is a perfect example of a dystopia that pretends to be a utopia. The government believes that without color, emotion, and feeling, the world will be a safer place. The leaders think that erasing these things will keep mankind at peace. All it really does is **deprive** people of key aspects of human life.

Governments in Popular YAL

Two popular novels show just how far a government will go in a dystopian society. Imagine having to marry someone chosen for you by a computer program. What would happen if there were an error? What if you were accidentally matched to the wrong partner? In Ally Condie's Matched trilogy, a computer error causes the protagonist to rethink her entire life. She later rebels against her controlling government.

In Marie Lu's *Legend*, the government tests all children. Then, the leaders use the results to decide what the children's roles in life will be. The highest-scoring children are trained to lead the military. The lowest-scoring children are used for medical experiments.

All Governments Aren't Bad!

There are some novels that do not have corrupt governments. Instead, natural disasters cause life to change suddenly. Citizens and governments must work together to fight the elements and survive. In Susan Beth Pfeffer's *Life As We Knew It*, an asteroid hits the moon. The moon moves closer to Earth. This causes natural disasters such as earthquakes, tsunamis, exploding volcanoes, and terrible storms. Survival becomes difficult. In this novel, the government tries to help people. It tries to give the people what they need to survive.

Trilogy, Trilogy, Trilogy

Many dystopian trilogies share common storylines. In most cases, the first novel is where the protagonist realizes he or she is living in a corrupt world. In the second novel, the main character takes a journey, goes into hiding, or is thrown into combat. The final novel concludes the story and ends in the resolution or defeat of the conflict or government.

Rebellious Teens

In most dystopias, young adults fight against the system to change corrupt worlds. Each of these teen's stories begins in different stages of their lives. Some characters are lost, confused, and lonely. Others may not know where they belong or how to survive. In the end, these teenagers realize they have the power to stop **tyranny** in their worlds.

These characters go through many tragic and life-changing events before reaching this conclusion. They often lose family or friends. This triggers their responses to the dystopian worlds. The teenagers may not seem like major threats to the establishment, but they are usually strong problem solvers with one goal in mind: to end the dystopia. Whether it is protecting a loved one, living just one more day, or escaping the terrible world they have known all their lives, each of these teens has reasons to rebel and fight against greater forces.

Why are so many dystopian protagonists teenagers? Teens are noted for being rebellious and risk takers. Plus, the age of the main character makes a big difference. Young adults like reading stories about young adults. The reader can feel empowered and inspired. Readers may believe they have the ability to change their own worlds.

Teens Aren't the Only Ones

Of course, there are adults who rebel in many of these books as well. An early dystopian book is Ray Bradbury's novel, *Fahrenheit 451*. In it, Montag spins his world out of control. He searches to understand the past and present.

THINK LINK

- In what ways do teens and adults behave differently in dystopias than in the normal world?
- How might governments underestimate the teen rebels in these books?
- If you were living in a dystopia, would you fight back or follow the crowd? Explain your answer.

Normal?

What is normal? Normal is usually considered average, proper, and what people are used to. Normal is nothing out of the ordinary. Many times, young adult characters are **abnormal** in some way. This makes them stand out. It draws others' attention to them.

Main characters who are abnormal may think differently from others. This special way of thinking can make them realize that the hardships of the world are unnecessary. This leads them to take action against the dystopian leaders.

Passion, creativity, and intelligence are common traits in young protagonists. They are loving people with tough exteriors. As readers get to know them, they realize how much the young adults care about their friends and family. They will do anything to protect those around them.

Gifted in Dystopia

Some gifted people think outside the box. They understand things in different ways from how others do. They have the capacities to change the world through words, music, mathematics, or movement. Gifted children today are often nurtured and challenged. But in dystopias, children are not given chances to challenge themselves, which leaves them with plenty of untapped potential.

Just Average

Not every young adult protagonist is abnormal. In *Life As We Knew It*, the main character is an ordinary girl. Yet she fights to save her family and herself as she conflicts with nature and society.

Strength in Numbers

Even the strongest and smartest protagonists in dystopian novels do not take on challenges alone. Friends, family members, and sometimes former foes help fight against the forces keeping people down.

Dig Deeper!

Diagram of Rebellious Teens

Young protagonists problem solve to figure out how they can change the world.

The rebels see the world from unique perspectives.

These young leaders love their families and friends. They will do almost anything to protect them.

Teen protagonists have to take deep breaths to remind themselves to stay calm and confident.

Mind Control Backfires

Creativity is a freedom. This freedom is **denied** to people in dystopias. Colors, emotions, and self-expression are threats. Allowing people to think freely gives them control. The idea of not being in control scares dystopian leaders. So they watch every part of peoples' lives. People are forced to follow routines. But, some characters ignore these routines. This creates conflict.

In YAL, teenage characters often fight against society's control. They want to be free. This is also true for dystopian novels. Characters must fight just to survive. In most young adult novels, survival is personal or emotional. In dystopian novels, survival is literal.

Unexpected Talents

Sometimes, characters do not mean to rebel. They end up in tough situations. Then, they accidentally discover new things. In *Red Queen* by Victoria Aveyard, Mare Barrow is surprised to discover that she has powers. This both **intrigues** and frightens her. It also frightens the government leaders.

Remember When...

The government can ban creativity, but it cannot entirely erase it from the past. In *The Giver*, the young protagonist discovers he is missing parts of life that previous generations had. He discovers how important it is to be creatively free.

Fight or Flight?

When **heroic** characters are given the choice to fall back into the crowd or fight, they usually fight. But a small number of them wants to slip back into the peaceful, **naive** state of childhood. Some young characters have experienced trauma, and they are so scared that they wish they could run away. They want to let the adults take on the heavy lifting.

This is true in most YAL. Young adults get scared and hope for somebody to save them. In *Divergent* by Veronica Roth, Tris faces this conflict. She tells herself that she *must* hide who she truly is to protect herself and her loved ones. However, she shows her true colors when she faces life-threatening tasks to help resolve her society's conflicts. Her brave instincts overcome her fear.

A controlling government is an intimidating force. It raises people to believe that safety, order, and no personal expression are best for society. But when people realize such control is unnecessary, the idea of a rebellion begins to stir. And at the head of the rebellion is often a young rebel leader.

Only So Many Options...

In dystopias, art may be erased from people's memories, or it is limited and very censored. This is true in *Matched*, where Cassia discovers a whole new world of stories, songs, poems, and paintings beyond the few that the government has allowed people to enjoy. Only 100 out of millions of art forms are allowed in her world.

Burning Books

Fahrenheit 451 is an excellent example of how a government brainwashes its citizens. In this novel, people are made to believe that books and creative thinking have caused all the problems in the world. Books, and anyone who owns them, are destroyed. People think this will protect them in the future.

The Spark That Triggers the End

What causes a character in a story to change the world? Usually, a major event happens as a spark, or **catalyst**. This event is often tragic. It pushes the teen protagonist into action. This single event creates a chain reaction that triggers other events. The initial spark makes the protagonist understand that he or she needs to rebel because life will not change without a fight.

Sparks are often the most dramatic parts of the stories. Death, sickness, betrayal, or abduction are all common sparks in dystopian novels. Once the spark ignites, there is no turning back. This event leads to the main conflicts and **climax** in the story.

A story's spark helps readers to better understand the protagonist. The young adult's reaction gives clues about his or her personality, morals, and beliefs. Understanding the protagonist helps readers predict what will happen next in the story.

The Wave That Sparks

In *The 5th Wave* by Rick Yancey, evil forces take Cassie's brother. This leads her to search for him, which drives the plot of the story. Her search creates a major individual vs. society conflict. This time, though, society is not a controlling leader or government—it's an alien race!

Family Ties

In *Legend*, the protagonists are June and Day. For each of them, the spark that begins the conflict relates to family. Their sparks bring them together. As a team, they fight the dystopian society in which they live.

Death as a Tragic Spark

Death is the most common spark to trigger action in a story. This is especially true when government neglect causes the death. But, fear, attack, addiction, injury, or kidnapping can also be a trigger. Characters may have families for whom they are responsible. Others must step up because their parents have died. Either way, a spark triggers the characters' next actions.

If both parents die, the protagonist is left to look after the family. Other times, he or she is sent to a dystopian orphanage. If one parent dies, the teen often feels closest to the dead parent. In some novels, the living parent grows too weak, ill, or sad to look after the family. That is what happens to Katniss at the start of the Hunger Games trilogy. She is forced to act.

Protecting and Providing

Another powerful spark in young adult literature is the drive to protect and provide for loved ones. America, the main character in Kiera Cass's *The Selection*, enters a competition. She competes to earn money for her family. The better she does, the more money her family receives. America's choices are driven by the needs of her loved ones.

Teen protagonists will often do anything to protect friends and family. They will even stand up to governments or groups that control many parts of their lives.

- What event in your life has sparked changes or a new direction?
- What other sparks can you name from dystopian books you've read?
- Why is it important for authors to choose tragic or powerful sparks in these novels?

Who Knows What's Out There?

In a dystopian world, government leaders may tell people that the outside world is a dangerous wasteland. But that is not always true. Many times, the corrupt leaders lie to keep peace and order. This prevents people from wandering beyond society's barriers. It allows the government to stay in control.

Leaders in these societies **instill** fear in people to keep them under control. Leaders want to keep citizens in line and prevent them from rebelling. This usually works. Most citizens are afraid of the "outside." But the protagonists often discover they are too curious to be afraid. Or, they find that they cannot live in the corrupt world any longer, no matter the consequences.

I'm Scared!

Fear is what keeps a corrupt government working. If its citizens are afraid of life beyond the barriers, they will look to the higher authority to protect them. People put their trust and faith in the government. This gives power to the dishonest leaders. Whether or not the outside world is truly destroyed, people become frightened of change and cling to the hand of the government for support.

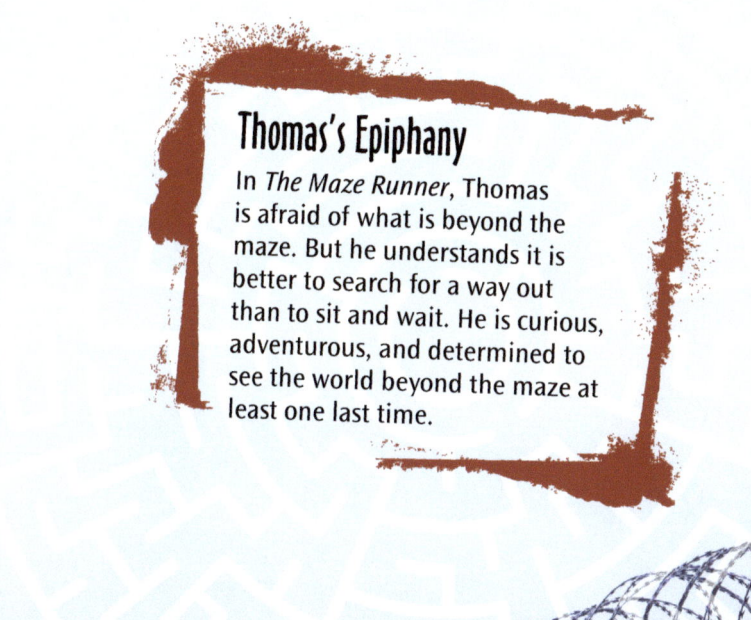

Thomas's Epiphany

In *The Maze Runner*, Thomas is afraid of what is beyond the maze. But he understands it is better to search for a way out than to sit and wait. He is curious, adventurous, and determined to see the world beyond the maze at least one last time.

Beyond Ugly Town

Uglies by Scott Westerfeld is a perfect example of a society unaware of the world beyond. This creepy book takes place in Uglyville and New Pretty Town. One major rule of Uglyville is for citizens to stay within the boundaries. Tally, the protagonist, knowingly ignores this rule and explores beyond the enforced limits.

Are people in these worlds truly afraid of the outside? Or are they afraid of losing protection? The government is so controlling that people find it comfortable. It covers them with a blanket of safety. The thought of giving that up for something unknown is horrifying.

The outside world is not always warm and fuzzy. The government cannot control things beyond its small areas of land. Within the boundaries of a country or city, everything can be controlled. The outside land is untamable and unfamiliar. Playing up the fear of the unknown is the perfect way to scare people.

Losing the **irrational** fear of the outside is one thing that sets the main character apart from the other citizens. Some characters are initially afraid of the unknown. Others grow up **skeptical** of the government's warnings. They ignore the government. Either way, these protagonists overcome their fears to face the bigger picture.

Decisions, Decisions

When the world beyond the city or country is a wasteland, characters have to decide whether to turn back and return to the unsafe but familiar origin. Most often, the fearsome path ahead is nowhere near as bad as the dystopian society behind them.

The Lights Are Going Out

In Jeanne DuPrau's *The City of Ember*, Lina and Doon live underground in a dystopian society. The lights of their city serve as a boundary for the citizens. Everyone is taught from an early age that to venture into the darkness means sure death. As the lights begin to fail, Lina and Doon must discover what is in the darkness.

Restricted Lives

Citizens in dystopian worlds have very little privacy. Their personal choices are unfairly restricted, which causes differences in **socioeconomic** levels. Unlike free societies, people in dystopias have limited career choices. They get stuck in one way of life.

Privacy is not only invaded in a dystopia; it is eliminated. Leaders believe that people should not have time to themselves. Citizens might think in ways that threaten the fragile society. They might realize what they are missing and start a **revolution**. Both of these could cause a **downfall** of the government. So, citizens are closely monitored.

When everything is chosen for you, is it really a fulfilling life? No. This scenario takes place in *Red Queen*. The world is completely controlled by the government. The government even makes the choices that citizens would usually decide on their own. In other novels, fences or walls surround characters, and they are often forced into exile.

Medicines

Drugs and medicines are sometimes used to keep people from changing the way they think about their world. In *The Giver*, medicine is used to prevent people from feeling emotions. Jonas begins to skip taking his medicine. This helps open his mind to a world of passion and color.

Helpful or Harmful?

In the Matched trilogy, Cassia is given three emergency pills—one blue, one green, and one red. The blue pill gives her nutrients to survive three days in the wild. The green pill calms her nerves, and the red pill erases memories. These three pills show how much control the government has on even the smallest aspects of life.

Where in the Real World?

Are there any traces of dystopia in the real world? These novels have touched the world in many ways. People today can connect to the novels they truly love through movies, merchandise, and more!

One of the most intriguing parts of dystopian novels for many is how they allow the reader to wonder where parts of the novel may take place in the real world. Authors often drop hints about these places within the text, but it is up to the readers to piece them together and discover the locations.

No matter where the stories are set, they all have one thing in common: the time frame. Even if it is only a few years, weeks, days, or hours into the future, these societies are not set in the present. While some authors give dates and times, others leave the readers in the dark.

This map shows one interpretation of how the districts of Panem might fit on a modern map of the United States.

Am I in District 12?

The country of Panem in *The Hunger Games* seems to be set in North America during an unnamed future. The districts each have certain goods they produce best. These goods are hints to where each district is located. For example, District 12 mines lots of coal, much like the Mid-Atlantic region today. And District 7 produces lumber, similar to modern-day Northern California.

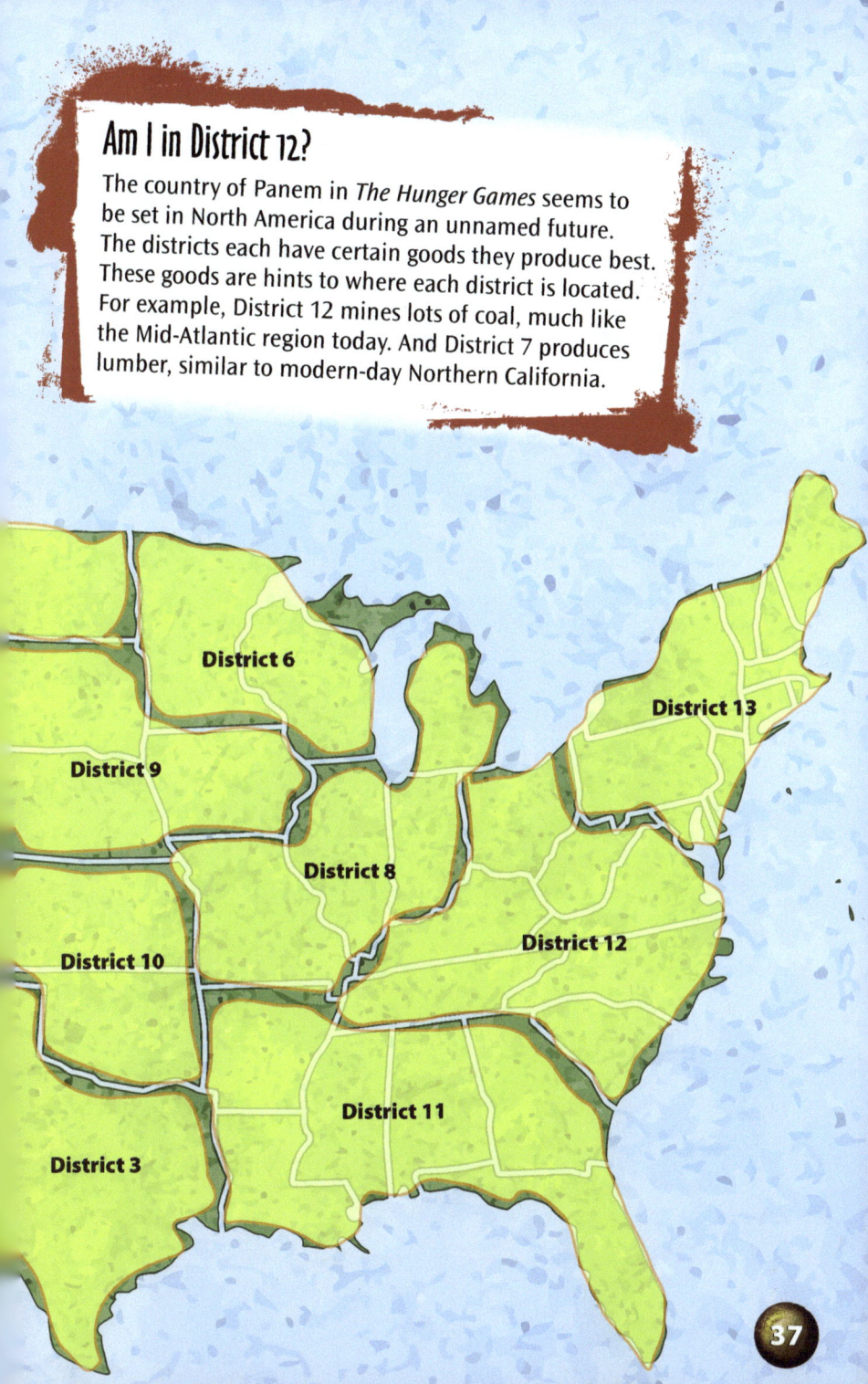

Heading to Hollywood

Many dystopian novels have been made into popular movies. The movies are filmed in places similar to the settings in the books. In some cases, the films are shot in the actual cities where the novels are set.

The film location is key to the success of a movie. Choosing the right settings can make a movie more like the novel. The settings can also create a sense of familiarity for the reader.

Today's special effects go a long way toward making the horrible dystopias real. Epic battles take place on wastelands that are actually green screens. Computerized explosions and other effects are used to create chaos.

Chicago is not only the home of Lake Michigan and the Chicago River. For book lovers, it is also where Tris and Four from the Divergent trilogy live. A *Divergent* fan in Chicago is like a kid in a candy store.

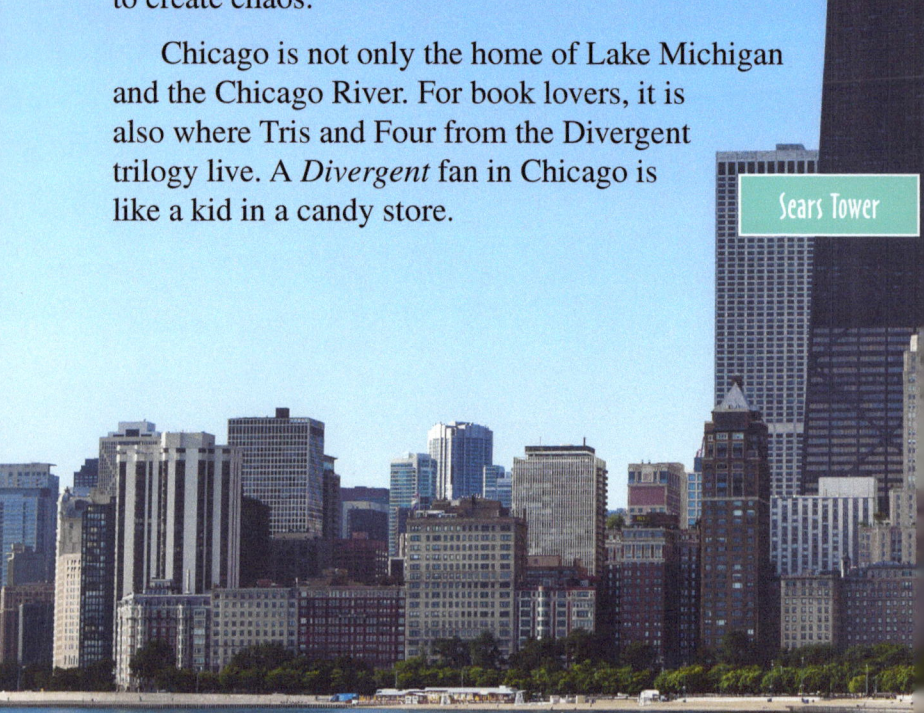

Sears Tower

Merchandise Mart

The Chicago L

The Bean

Navy Pier

STOP! THINK...

- How do readers discover where their favorite books take place?
- What do you notice about the Chicago locations that Veronica Roth uses in the Divergent series?
- What aspects of Chicago's location make it an ideal setting for a dystopian novel?

Gaming

In some cases, these novels cross over into more than just the Hollywood silver screen. The popular game *Minecraft* has caught the attention of many *Hunger Games* fans. Fans can use servers from the game to play versions of their own arena games. This allows different players to face one another. Players fight in domes where they have to find food and weapons. They also try to make allies.

Fandoms

Dystopian novels have become so popular they often have their own **fandoms**. A fandom is a group of people who share a mutual love and passion for a book, movie, or TV series. People in fandoms are usually familiar with both the written works and the films. They often feel closely attached to the characters and the stories.

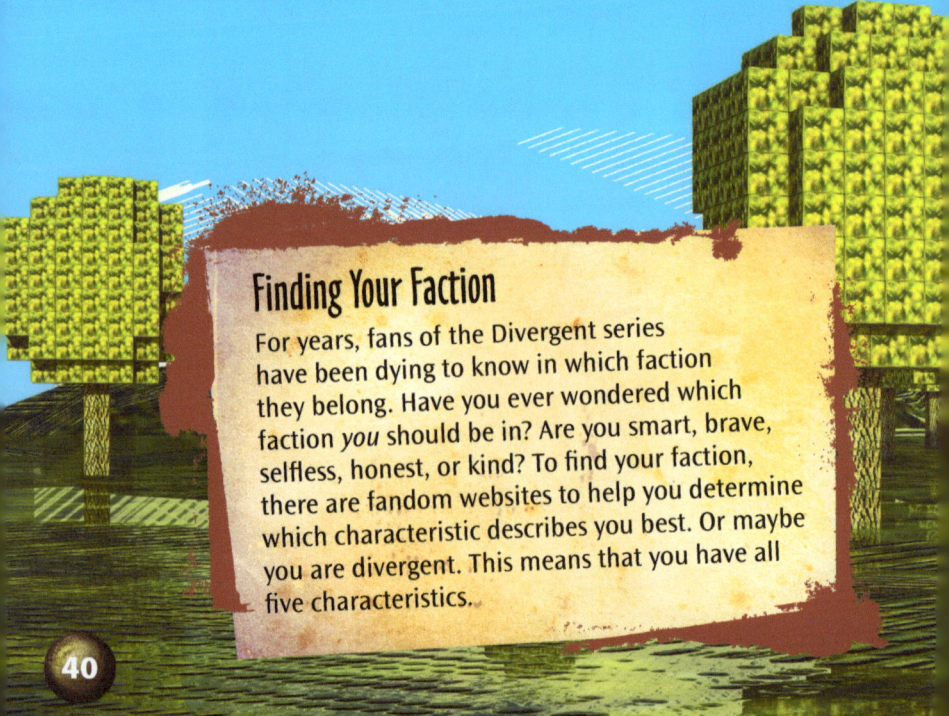

Finding Your Faction

For years, fans of the Divergent series have been dying to know in which faction they belong. Have you ever wondered which faction *you* should be in? Are you smart, brave, selfless, honest, or kind? To find your faction, there are fandom websites to help you determine which characteristic describes you best. Or maybe you are divergent. This means that you have all five characteristics.

Social Media and Fandoms

Many fans belong to more than one fandom. They talk and post about their fandoms on social media—A LOT. Members of fandoms sometimes create websites, write fan fiction, and personalize accounts on social media sites.

All's Fair in War and Utopia

The real world is not a utopia. On bad days, this world may sometimes seem as if it is heading toward a dystopia. But we have something that many characters living in YAL dystopian worlds do not—the freedom of choice.

As young adults read dystopian novels, they may feel empowered. They see that people can make a difference. They can stand up for what they believe. They can fight back or protect their loved ones. They have the choice to stand out and to express themselves creatively.

In dystopian novels, the protagonists wage epic battles or wars to defeat the societies, individuals, or forces of nature that limit them. However, these battles are unrealistic resolutions. In reality, there will always be evil. It does not end with one war, one death, or one battle. In the real world, it does not end when the book is over because the book of life never truly closes.

Young adults need to look at the world around them and help create a planet that is closer to utopia than dystopia. Because in a way, if people do have a choice, we are already in a utopia.

Desperate Times

It is said that "Desperate times call for desperate measures." Many people still believe that war is the solution to our problems. In dystopian novels, that's often the case. Is it true in the real world?

Glossary

abnormal—different from average; uniquely different
catalyst—something that causes change
climax—the most intense point in a story; before the resolution
conceal—to hide
corrupt—dishonest; evil; unkind; manipulative
denied—prevented from having something
deprive—to prevent others from having something
discord—disagreement between people and ideas
downfall—destruction; loss of power
dystopia—a fictional place where citizens are unhappy and afraid
fandoms—groups of people who share a mutual love and passion for a book, a movie, or a series
foreseeable—able to be predicted
heroic—showing great courage
instill—gradually cause
intrigues—interests deeply
irrational—not logical
naive—innocent
necessities—things you must do
prosperity—the state of being successful
protagonists—important main characters in stories who make good choices
revolution—rebellion against a governing force
skeptical—doubtful
socioeconomic—related to social and economic factors
tyranny—unfair treatment
utopias—fictional places where citizens are happy and safe

Index

5th Wave, The, 27
Aveyard, Victoria, 22
Bradbury, Ray, 16
Cass, Kiera, 28
Chicago, 38–39
Cinder, 7
City of Ember, The, 33
Condie, Ally, 14
Dashner, James, 7
Divergent, 24, 38–40
DuPrau, Jeanne, 33
Fahrenheit 451, 16, 25
Giver, The, 13, 23, 34
Hunger Games, The, 28, 37, 40
Legend, 14, 27
Life As We Knew It, 14, 18
Lowry, Lois, 13
Lu, Marie, 14

Matched, 14, 24, 35
Maze Runner, The, 31
Meyer, Marissa, 7
Minecraft, 40
Panem, 36–37
Pfeffer, Susan Beth, 14
Red Queen, 22, 34
Roth, Veronica, 24, 39
Scorch Trials, The, 7
Selection, The, 28
Uglies, 31
Yancey, Rick, 27
Westerfeld, Scott, 31

Check It Out

Listed below are the series and books from this reader as well as others you may be interested in checking out!

Aveyard, Victoria—Red Queen series
Bradbury, Ray—*Fahrenheit 451*
Cass, Kiera—The Selection series
Collins, Suzanne—The Hunger Games series
Condie, Ally—Matched series
Dashner, James—Maze Runner series
DuPrau, Jeanne—Book of Ember series
Haddix, Margaret Peterson—Shadow Children series
Lowry, Lois—The Giver Quartet
Lu, Marie—Legend series
Meyer, Marissa—The Lunar Chronicles
Meyer, Stephenie—*The Host*
Oliver, Lauren—Delirium series
Orwell, George—*1984*
Pfeffer, Susan Beth—Last Survivors series
Roth, Veronica—Divergent series
Westerfeld, Scott—Uglies series
Yancey, Rick—The 5th Wave series

Try It!

You have been asked to develop a storyboard for a major motion picture company about a dystopian society. Where will your society be located? How can you make this movie different from its predecessors?

- Begin by making a map and naming your dystopia. How will the population be divided, and why?

- Who will lead your dystopia? One leader? A group? What aspects of life are they going to control? What event triggered the leaders to hold all the power?

- What prompts the protagonist to become involved? How are others inspired to join the fight?

- How is power given back to the people in the end? In what ways is the new world better?

- Use your ideas to create your storyboard by hand or digitally. If you have time, you can even take it a step further and turn your storyboard into a short video using online sites or apps!

About the Author

Kiley E. Smith is a middle schooler from Virginia. She's passionate about writing and maintains a blog of her work. She enjoys acting, singing, and playing volleyball. However, her favorite extracurricular activity is basketball. Kiley has played basketball since second grade and hopes to play through college. She has had poems and stories published in various books and on blogs. This is Kiley's first full book.